Published November 2023

Wagram, NC

"What it is that made the soil is still a mystery. To explain its origin is probably equivalent to explaining the origin of life itself."

— Nikola Tesla, in *The Problem of Increasing Human Energy, With Special Reference to the Harnessing of the Sun's Energy*

Dedicated to all my good neighbors.

(Not you, guy who stole our rooster, if you're reading this; you can go to hell.)

If you don't like poetic things
You may not like this book.
And if you do, you still may not.
But have a heart to look.

CONTENTS

ONE ACT

One act of creation always
Will lead to another.
When there is a stop there's only
The stagnant old water.

One moment, though loose and fleeting,
Becomes a good mother;
One step of a crude excreting,
The seminal father.

One chain is unbroken, though we
May frown at a link;
One river you swim in with me,
Whatever you think.

STARTING BOY

Starting boy, drink up, strap on,
Stepping out all sure and strong,
Striking off to make yourself
Stories you one day will tell.

Twists and turns ambush, arise,
Ringing ears and stinging eyes.
Story bags fill up with filth,
Holding glee or holding guilt.

Half he dumps and throws away;
Half he hides till Judgement Day.
All a man brings back to share,
A joke, half-truth, or odd affair.

Here and there they'll hear one right,
But all the best are out of sight.
He'll never be convinced to tell;
Old men don't want to go to hell.

DON'T CALL A POET

Don't call a poet "genius"—
The two are poles apart
     (Though not all geniuses are right
     And not all poets have a heart).

Most geniuses are celibate
     (Or nearly so, it seems);
A poet's more promiscuous
     (If only in his dreams).

PLANT GOOD DEEDS

Plant good deeds
As if they're seeds
Because they are
They grow what you need
And branch out far

Sometimes you need to go around
Sometimes, please stop, don't chop it down
Plant where you can, you're not in charge
Living in nature is living large

Time gives more
It's what life's for
And one man's sin
Another's manure
To put seeds in

HALLOWED HERE

We murmur how we got here
From upstream in a linear way
Ah, no words may convey
How reality is more circular

Ah, the hallowed here
The sacred place today
A holy hush is hovering
Birdsong floats on timeless breath

IN WAGRAM WOODS

In Wagram woods I'll get my goods
        My kernel of creation
        My nut to give a nation

When walking there in sacred air
        I'll find the breath of elohim
        Inhale afresh and sun the skin

With water oak and sassafras
And pine, redbay and willow
The berries, walnuts, wild grass
And mosses for a pillow
The sweetgum and some pawpaw fruit
The maple and mulberry
The holly and magnolia
And hickory and cherry

        Like a dog whose bone is there—
                No, a cat with a water fetish
        Or a fish with a taste for air
                How can one comprehend my forest?
        Though it's not like I won't share

I'll blink and link the earth and sky
Then sleep to meet my maker
In Wagram woods I'll live and die
And bless the undertaker

RAIN SONG DRUMS

Rain song drums on the roof
White strings, they strum into the earth
Like whiskers on a wizard beard
No saying what his song is worth

Another steamy night
She told me it was like
Buckets of sunshine gold
Pouring upon her soul

Water is life, life is beauty
What else is good and true?

Money men muddy waters
Praying not to drown
Their form secure in dead ugliness
Like default orange vests
Regulators of life jackets
Upward floats an urge to yawn
Or in better moments
To laugh

But water

Water is the fountain

Not so safe

Fountain of life crashing back down

Flow of a sunshine gold

Blood of Love

True religion

Real life

Real life drums on the roof

Life is water, life is truth

SOME MOTION

Some motion, friction, heat
Fill a year, or ten
Fill a body, fill a book
Till you ask, "What then?"

And then, when life moves on
Energy will build
Heat arising into light
Till the eyes are filled

Some light, some burning life
Fill a timeless eye
Years and books and bodies pass
Light will never die

THOSE WHO THINK

Those who think that English
Is a high and delicate art
Curse the ways I've used it,
The cruder fruits of the heart.

      They'll shake a finger,
      Write their quips,
      Cross their arms
      And purse their lips.

      Older tongues (which they forget, I guess)
      Make fewer stops and squeaks.

Their opinionated lips may kiss
My crude and hairy cheeks.

IF ONE BREATH

If one breath
Were my due
Chance to say
Words to you
Then I might
Look your way
Clear my throat
Slowly say
Just six words
Not too rude
"You can grow
Your own food."

SNAKING VINES

Snaking vines all through the mind
Tangle, twist and tie
Knots around the thoughts to bind
Right to left and earth to sky.

Chestnut used to reach the sun
Through a tangled mass;
Now it's ragged or pine or gum,
Not so tasty, growing fast.

Fertile mind or fertile ground
Feeds the winding vines
Growing through and all around
Shifting flavors, changing times.

GARDENS

How stunningly mesmerizing
Have been the well-groomed gardens of
Civilizations under cultivation,
How fascinating the sculpted life forms
Contained and constrained therein,
How clean-cut with trim edges.

How valiantly inspired were tireless fights
To keep the dark old jungles from returning;
How relentlessly man pruned back to nothing
The ancient snaking vines.

How amazing have been gardens'
Expanding new blooms, mushrooming
From murder to rape to slavery to war.
How multicolored grew those hungry flowers,
So much more neatly in order than
Tangled old jungles
Of naked Eden.

DO YOU HAVE LIFE?

Do you have life?
      Crack a smile.
Do you have legs?
      Walk a mile.
Body and mind?
      Clap your hands.
Walls and a roof?
      Bless our lands.
People to love?
      What a thing!
Eyes? Ears? A mouth?
      Open, sing.
Water and food?
      Chew it slow.
Do you have life?
      Watch it grow.

IN THE WALNUT NEIGHBORHOODS

In the walnut neighborhoods
Of my little Wagram woods
Neighbors like their elbow space.
You can smell throughout the place
How some pushed and shoved about,
Elbow nudged each other out.
Their effect, though, on the whole
Makes a place where I can stroll.

So they've grown, exhaled their scent,
And I follow where they went,
Breathing in their clearing spots,
Cracking open human thoughts.
And their nuts I'll share one day
(Or I'll try to anyway)
Just as long as neighbors give
Space to breathe and peace to live.

LIQUID LYRICS

Liquid lyrics, wicked fruits
Licked a spirit, tasting juice
      Tongue gone wilder
      Purpose served
      Then got milder
      Rosy words

Yet I cannot settle
For penning dry red lines
Thus no mild or settled love
Can be a muse of mine

Heaven's boring; so is love
      When exploring's given up.
Though love will last a lifetime,
      The muse will come and go:
Recurring dripping lifeline,
      A wilder, freer flow.

DÉJÀ VU

Déjà vu leans, bending through sound
Memory moonbeams vibrate the ground
Never giving in to silence
Even when besieged in violence
Even through humiliations
Beaming sound for generations
Saving, never let it melt
Never giving up, I felt
Even though we write in English
Word and sound may be distinguished
From each other, pulling, playing
Bend some memories for relaying

CHRONOLOGICAL ORDER

Chronological order settles
Into a rhythm you know
Linear pattern of story spells
Letters' familiar flow
      Comforting if a rain is chilly
      Or when a breeze is harsh
      Unmoving surfaces clean and still
         Unlike a windy marsh

Chronological warm illusion
Dry when it's baked in the sun

         Underneath is a looping infusion
         Where the old muddy ways run

JOSÉE'S HAWK

Some define themselves by their losses,
Others by a gain or winning play.
Some folks write their words for a living;
Others live to write and give away.

Yesterday she saw a gliding hawk
Whose motion wrote what all the words could not.
Wins and losses felt so far below
The wordless athlete in dynamic thought.

Look and look, then dive to a banquet,
Swoop, attack, and reap a little runt.
Back again to soar over treetops.
Others may define; he'll only hunt.

APPETITE

Poking around within
This or that head;
Whirling, we swoop and spin,
Peck divine bread.

                              Yet we are not two birds,
                                    Nor a whirlwind.
                              Biting my broken words
                                    Has to give in.

Whether you like or not,
You're a human,

                  Hunting, craving, like me,
                  Heaping helpings of love.

                        Alright.
                  I may have a hidden stash.
                        Wait here a bit
                        And gradually
                  I'll dish you up a plate.

ODD DAYDREAM

Parched, I yesterday imagined
Life's no easy feast, but famine.
And a preacher stern confirmed it:
"Earth's no banquet; none have earned it."

And he blew his wind,
        His holy truth,
To arrest the play
        Of lowly roots.
Celebrations damp
        Got brittle, dried,
And a piece of God
        Curled up and died.

The daydream was too odd
And found an end,
So join me here in God,
My feasting friend.

USED PAPER

Smooth out a wrinkled-up paper,
Each crease and rip a story trip.
Run a hand gently over where
Rough-surface memories slip,

Roughly used page of yourself,
Sliding fingers tenderly, sense
A rustle of life and hope.
Blow off the dust of arrogance.

That wrinkle was shuddering shock,
This one a spot where blood was spilt;
Up here runs a ripping loneliness,
And down here lies a simmering guilt.

Smooth out the wrinkles with care.
Turn it over, look to find
An empty space of blankness there;
I may use it, if you don't mind.

WHO?

Who violated her?

Who refused her the right kind of love
And gave her something else instead?

Who stole from humanity
In the physical form of her?

And who first violated that violator?
Who first refused that future refuser?
Who first stole from the fledgling thief?
How far back does the chain go?
Who gave birth and raised the anti-love?

Don't give me that mama.
I want this one...

But not in that way.
Not to violate, refuse, steal.

Maybe it'll be easier to see what I mean
When I'm a sagging ninety years old,
Empty of lust, and when

She won't want me that way either.

But who will love her?

BROKEN MIRRORS

Even if you find yourself
In these shards on my old shelf,
No one's going shopping for
Broken mirrors at the store.

No illusions cloud this head;
Poems will not earn my bread.
Puzzle pieces form your eyes,
Smiling face, my silent prize.

Teachers may not see my name
In their lessons. Just the same,
Words may get inflated by
How their writers go and die.

Never mind, just look in here.
Eye to eye, you lose your fear.
Alive or dead, I'll never mind
What broken mirrors come to find.

CELEBRATING

This one note at least
May translate into any human tongue
Rhyme and rhythm be damned
Laying aside melody and harmony of sound
Look for a moment
How a dancing thicket of reeds
Watches every sunset without fail
And never seems to tire of celebrating!
So, what if a passerby with
More lizard brain than human sense
Interrupts our dance?
If he's hungry let's feed him anyway
Laughing off his unfairness
Laughing because of all those chuckling sunsets
Because even if goodness doesn't end up winning
It's worth celebrating anyway

SHOW ME

Show me your passion, I'll give it a voice
Bring me your fire and I'll show you a choice
Give me your pain, I won't write it away
Open your hope in the light of this day

Why am I sitting and writing these lines?
When will you see how your face is divine?
Uncork a bottle you have from above
Give me your passion, I'll give you my love

ISN'T THAT WAY

Sometimes death goes like this:
If you hesitate, you die.

But life isn't that way.

Sometimes color goes like this:
If you keep moving, you miss it.

But light isn't that way.

Sometimes mind goes like this:
If you don't understand, you get mad.

But joy isn't that way.

THAT FACE WAS

That face was
> Voracious
>> Tenacious
> Too hungry
>> Or horny

Adjectives stuck where the sermons were thorny

> "Right, not left
> Up, not down
> Dress right, dress
> Square, not round"

Bit shallow, bit literal, earnestly hollow
Staking a "place" beyond time so we follow
But trust and obey was a way to atrocity
Tone down the mouth, better check the velocity

Make my escape with the hastily scattered
Eating some shapes that allegedly mattered

Fit in a rank and a file if you like it
Flank 'em and move if you think you can hike it

Failing to swim in a place

All mud-spattered

Fast personality face

Till it shattered

NATURE HAS PREFERRED

Nature has preferred
The thriving of the more harmonious types;
Yet she has decreed
Some plants will be invasive,
As will some animals, like this sort of people.

      Don't get all worked up.
      Nature's giggling.
      Control is a funny game;
      Play it if you like
      But then think,
      "What sort am I being?"

She can enjoy both,
And do more than giggle
When invasions happen.
      We men must be humble because
      God exists more powerfully within
      A female orgasm.

EARLY OR LATE

"Early to bed, early to rise"
Protects a man from poetry;
To ludicrous lines and lust of the eyes
He builds a bland immunity.

      Then others prefer a lazier way,
      Declining to rise and fight the fight.
      They lie in the bed for half of the day,
      Make anti-poetic noise at night.

Down with your hand, there is no key;
Hold your own answerless questions.
Better find someone wiser than me
If looking for moderate lessons.

THERE WAS

There were only
Swirling
Humming
Colors
And then there
Was light up there
And there was I
Like a miniscule wildflower bud
Unfolding, unfolding, endlessly
Toward the light
Bending, twisting, reaching
Rising taller, opening up toward
The light, light, light
Expand oh expand me to the light
There was an unfolding without end
And then
There was the light in me
And there
Was Everything

MISTY DREAM

You and I were jointly a type
Of Noah last night, but more fun,
With room for a few more animals—
Mostly the lively human ones.
We floated over the ivy walls
Of Eden with gates still shut
And bobbing on the surface there
Were fruits for us to pluck,
Their seeds to germinate so easily
In all the mist and raining down
Of the flooding of everything else—
Greed and jealousy seemed to drown....
Then I woke and started the day,
And the mist began to clear.
Before it all evaporated,
I had to write something here.

ANTHROPOMORPHISM

I vote for you, your freedom,
Not judging if you're feeling
The key out of a prison
Is anthropomorphism.
But isn't it odd
If a person-like God
Has a face and a gender
      Yet never has sex?

This here's tangy space
To which a body may escape
When once the One under our feet
Does all the thinking to create.

To live out there is toxic.
Great love is therapy, you know.
Property is poisonous
But sharing is an antidote,
And so we'll share from time to time
A face or voice or pronoun for
The deity we know can shine
From dirt or bodies, mine or yours.

Who told you earth and heaven
       Are separate states of being?
Earth gave that person lemons
       But seeing is believing.

       Outside of skin and of physics,
              When death and time are gone,
              What movement corresponds
       To a heaven contained in this?

A mouth expounding "afterlife"
While frowning on heavenly here
Has failed to taste the lemons right;
I vote for the God that's near.

SIMPLE PEACE

Simple peace lay cool and easy

On young Francis of Assisi

With no rugrats and no mouthy mother-in-law.

So with clarity and gladness,

Standing free of family madness,

He took joy in every quiet dawn he saw.

A GROWER'S MOTION

From youth down to the grave
A grower's motion ought to be
To nurture her that gave
And save for future progeny.

    "I came, I saw, I gave"
    And opted not to ruin her.
    This place was made to save,
    Not strip away what grew in her.

In kindness to the land
Deposit more than you withdraw.
May every tribe and band
Pay heed to this eternal law.

    My movements, kind or rude,
    Flow into her from gratitude;
    My half-digested food,
    And thoughts and moods and attitude.

        When all my motion's calmed
        Then lower me down into her
        (Not burnt, boxed up, embalmed).
        Donate my body clean to her.

DRIP, DRIP, DRIP

Drip, drip, drip
Unpunctuated quiet measured
Now allow every syllable
Of silence
To drip
Drip
Drip
Onto the tongue
Down into the wound
Which is a throat sore from babbling
About what I thought I knew

The swallowing of pride is a difficult pill
A hasty gulp won't keep it down long enough
For love to burp out
For some, it never sinks home until
In gurgling bubbles of death

"God" and "Love" are listed somewhere
As synonyms in someone's lexicon
So let the petty tyrannies be a laugh

And what's to be gained

Reaching back for youthful days

The waves and haze of sweet testosterone

King Ego on a throne

So easy to forget

The throne's legs were uneven

The whole picture off-kilter

How easy a target I make of myself

(You have your own out-on-a-limb)

But may our green wood hold strong

With the sap of giving Love

Not brittle like bully boys

Who've learned to give no goodness

But rather trade in certain beliefs

Not swallowing their own spit

In quiet to let some

Silly little syllables

Drip

Drip

Drip

EYES

"Please avert from me your eyes,"
Begs the angst of one, and I
Automatically oblige.

"Give the penetrating gaze,"
Someone's open posture says;
I reluctantly engage.
So we risk poetic days.

What a baffling wonder I feel.
Though while masses of us comprise
A machine of hideous steel,
Yet Beauty herself lies in your eyes.

What insanity is this of mine,
Producing stacks of poems in a time
When eyes would rather die than read a book,
Buffoons would rather shout than stop and look.

No matter. What's to be done?
Leave it be.
Just let me
(If you please and if it's fun)

Look at you,
You look at me.

FOR THAT ONE JEHOVAH'S WITNESS

You shine a light of loving care
For people who
In darkness might lose hope, despair.
So, thanks to you.
Your group of purpose and of faith
Is standing out.
I thank you for a smiling face
That doesn't shout.

And yet your light, it seems to me,
Is pushing on
With such a heavy certainty
To go beyond
Where answers cannot naturally
Be written down,
Where mystery stands more casually
On holy ground.

Your Father's true and full of worth,
But some forget
The Mother Earth who gave me birth
And knows you yet.
We stand above her beating heart,

And at our feet,
We've shut her up in pavement hard
To make a street
And drive our ways of sunlight sure,
Like knowing all,
Forgetting how the earth is pure
Before the Fall.

      (Often in error
      Never in doubt
      Breathe cleaner air
      Feel it out)

I thank you, friend, for seeing my
Quite childish rhyme,
And hope to see a free reply
In ripened time.

PLUNK AND SWOOSH

Plunk and swoosh
Trickle, sweep and plunk
Paddling up a zigzag creek
Till the sun has sunk

Twilight dips
In between the trunks
Branches bend to brush your hair
Beavers take a dunk

Whirlpool whips
Play between the logs
Gurgle over sandbar lips
Clear some mental clogs

Motion goes
Through a tunnel green
Fluid flows and thoughts abate
Lighter ways are seen

A LUMBEE RIVER HAZE

A Lumbee River haze
Anointing summer days
In morning exhales a fertile breath
Like vapory tales of life and death.
The river's winding ways
Awake in daybreak haze.

A fog in ancient woods
Condensing nature's goods,
Refreshing and light, it brings the night
Out into the day to set aright
A thirsty lonesome leaf
Now dripping in relief.

From down below the eyes
You see the dew arise,
A scattered and softer sunlight here,
Like spirited drifting far and near.
Don't shy or shift your gaze
From Lumbee River haze.

SEEKING

Seeking, seek to know
Knowing, begin to forget
Forgetting, become a child
To childishly seek again

Clear enough, the circle closes
A fragile loop indeed
Broken only by that virus
That people know as greed

Greedy for correctness
Or for control
For "others" to admire us
A separate soul

Greedy for the pleasures
The sticky sweets
Shortcut little treasures
The easy cheats

If you want a shortcut
Here it is

Seeking, seek nothing
Knowing, know nothing
Forgetting, be nothing
A child of a cleared-out mind

FORGIVENESS, LIKE LOTION

Forgiveness, like lotion,

Might soothe an emotion,

Assuage irritation,

And tame inflammation.

Forgiving connection

Prevents an infection

But doesn't go far

In smoothing the scar.

At least let it tame

The worst of the blame

And maybe at best

Put anger to rest.

A scar that may linger

You feel with a finger,

Like holding a treasure

Of worth beyond measure.

WHY DO PEOPLE

"Why do people talk so much?
Why not write instead?"
Please excuse this ugly gripe
Nagging in my head.

"Why must talk go crowding out
Simpler streams of mind?"
Through my screen of melody,
This ugliness I find.

Hopefully these uglier lines
Soon will find an end,
Written out and put to bed
So I may be a more
        Harmonious friend.

(THIS ONE'S NOT FOR EVERYONE)

Hey girl,
(This one's not for everyone)
Hey girl,
Now I'm in your head.
You know I never pull out.

Return to your own man if you want,
But when he touches you,
Your mind will turn to me,

And I'll be there
Till you find
Over time

Your belly swells with
My meaning,
His love,
Our creations,
Everyone's new life.

TAKE IT EASY

Take it easy with me today

No need to go below the belt

We're only here, two bits of mind

Hearing you breathe

Seeing your soul

Feeling you

Speak

I'll listen

Being open

Taking it easy

COLLECTOR OF ITEMS

That one...

> Collector of items in gunslinger culture
> An ad infinitum mechanical vulture

But why feel that I'm any better than him?
The books are my items (their worth a bit dim)
I pick from cadavers, decaying old scenes
I act like they matter, my pickings of dreams
Collecting old stories that close with "The End"
And thinking, "It's not really over, my friend"
Some evenings, the brain is a burden and curse
Then others, I go on collecting each verse

Like this one...

LIKE THE WHIRLING

Like the whirling dervishes of Hafiz,
Like a misty wind at night,
Like a swinging acrobat on trapeze,
A beauty swirls and holds the sight.

Like a timeless rustling noise in the trees,
Like a laugh so sweet it hurts,
Like a voice of water, hum of the bees,
An ear will hear the song in spurts.

No offense to other senses, but
The eye and the ear connect so fine.
What better use of day or night
Than soaking in sound and sight divine?

ONCE THE LADY EROS HAD TWO SONS

Once the lady Eros had two sons.
Satisfaction was the older one,
      But his brother Passion always came in first.
Others called him "Pass"—he always did.
He would fly by "Sat", the slower kid,
      And in doing so he'd work up quite a thirst.

But Sat knew better when to stop.
He'd climb a hill, enjoy the top
      To gather up his breath and focus long.
One day, Pass joined him there; but for
The fun, they played some tug-of-war.
      Their mama looked and sang a wordless song.

Pulling there atop the hill,
He who won might take a spill,
      Tumbling back and down into the thorns.
Watching them just like a hawk,
Eros sat upon a rock,
      Wedged her tune into the air like horns.

As each one found his edge,
"Keep pulling" was his pledge

And so their game goes on and on today.

And still their mama sits

And hums her song in fits

Of laughter as she glories in their play.

FROM THIS BEND OF THE RIVER

From this bend of the river
The deepest darkest water
Is bound to overflow a bucket
Of man-made order

Propriety will burst at the seams
Moral meanings fray and fail
Metered rhymes all buckle in time
A weight to crack the trivial pail

Like marks and dots give up their spots
Finely crafted P's and Q's
Blow away in a breath of life
Exhaled downstream when a muse
Appears
A beat will skip the ears
Color ignore the eyes to go
Straight to the marrow
Deeper, darker
Streaming black water
May never release her secrets

What use is a broken bucket

Or spilled lyrics
Watering the weeds

What use are the weeds
Stared at by a man when he
With a barely audible grunt ceased
Sat dazed with eyes glazed
Clouded over, loud memories where
Shots rang, shouts were horrid
Someone fell in the weeds and dirt
Until dark water flowed over it all
And deep time flowed on

NOT EVERY TREE TAKES ROOT

Not every tree takes root
Some dry up and die
To transplant is a touchy task
But some will risk it
  Some will try

Not every poem sticks
Some will be a flop
For self-expression is a reach
When each of us will
  One day stop

"All or nothing" is a load of bull
Growing is a heavy numbers play
Weeding is a wasting of the time
But planting seeds may save the day

To add and not subtract
Take root and not to fall
To find a rhythm others miss
To risk the time is
  Worth it all

SOME MEN WILL ALWAYS

Some men will always run the race—
      Striving of the will to beat
The lunatic below the waist.
      Some, to prove a point, will put
That little rascal in his place.

      But where his place is, that's the rub.
      A spouse may tell you where—
      Yet how can one who's never run
      Your race sincerely know or care?
      The little man extends your life,
      But makes it harder, too;
      Prolongs your days but claims the nights
      (As matrimony hopes to do).

Oh, what to do? Oh, what is sin?
      Back and forth so hard we run.
To take him out or put him in?
      Keep him down or have some fun?
Well, don't ask me. We'll never win.

UNFINISHED CONVERSATION

Animal Instinct lay indolently
Under a sycamore, cool as could be,
Eating an apple right down to the core,
Barely a thought to get up or get more.

"Instinct's for animals; come on, grow up,"
Chided a Thought to him, heated and tough.
"Always you're lounging beneath an old tree
Like work is beneath you, like everything's free!"

Instinct was silent—no answer was made.
Reaching a leg to the edge of the shade,
He scraped little dents with the heel of his boot
Down in the ground by the sycamore roots.
He nestled each apple seed down in its place,
Then turned to the Thought with a smile on his face.

YOU FOUND OTHER STEPPINGSTONES

You found other steppingstones
Across the same old creek that winds.
Steps begin, bare and alone,
A sense I bear in clunky lines.

But sense impressions carried here —
Bare perceptions buried deep —
Mean nothing if they won't adhere
To human mystery you keep

Close to home within your mind
Where your feet are wet,
Where you and I were intertwined
Long before we met.

AN INTERLUDE

An interlude was whispered by roots today
Something of motion and repose
Poetry pausing for prose, a landing on a stairway
A path may tolerate a bench
Of still reflection

What is it, this Thing latent within all beauty?

Every scientist knows
That infinity exists
And yet our fixation with beginnings and ends
No, everything fixed is only to send us
An interlude

Some mathematicians even know
That goodness, unlike greed, is infinite

Have I learned my nation's equation yet?
How greed plus freedom equals loneliness

Back to what the old rugged roots whispered
How slow motion and wisdom may
Come with a nation's older age, or a person's

And something of a restless young buck

After a passionate death finding peace

In new life free of confused memory

Something in duality, attachment and repulsion

Then graduation from tyrannical pairs, pairings...

The all-permeating essence of each pure and powerful mode of force—that Essence is greater than the mode itself.

The spirit inherent in impulses of creation, procreation— that Spirit is greater than the impulses themselves.

The acts and sensations of love, though great, are inferior to the Life that animates and moves through them.

The body and its passions, though divine, are lower than the Substance that surrounds and lies within them all.

And these lower things are beautiful steppingstones. These accessible instincts are steps up a spiral stairway.

And you've got to begin somewhere honest.

FOR CHILDREN A NAP

For children
A nap is a dreaded penalty
Like being sent to bed may be
The end of the world.

Mature ones
Feel that death is an awful dream
Like turning off the light will mean
The end of all life.

But when tired, both young and older
Seek to rest in peace and be
Put out of the misery
Of further activity.

We shall see
"Gwelwn ni"
How it feels to lie down
For a nap inside the ground.

SOME POEMS OF PLACE

Some poems of place
In particular facing
Out there and not here
Make a difficult hearing
In globalist air
Where the root may be tearing
Incestuous tricks
To dilute when they're mixing
And transplanting men
Like transplanting lemons
May heal as they go
To grow the new poems
An immigrant's child
Who heard them not smiling
While growing in place
A future was facing

YET ONE LAST

Yet one last youthful time
Let it surge, the ancient burn.
Before they turn a page of mine,
Receive the ego in his turn.

> "I—I am alive—alive—
> Hellfire flares as I arrive..."

The servant at your feet
Was the barbarian at the gate.
The "me" that people meet
Became the "I" the good ones hate.

> "I am the vigor in your fury,
> The speed behind a hurry,
> A pang of nameless fright,
> A burning in the night,
> An urgency of lust,
> A potency, a thrust,
> The bass of panthers' growl,
> The sniper on the prowl;
> I am the reaper at the dawn;
> I am the death that's burning on."

"In your soul, your kernel of life
Before you were born, I am your strife."

But oh, may striving cease
And turn a page to blank-and-clean,
For restless blood to rest in peace
And pure-in-heart be felt and seen.

RUNNING COUNTER

Running counter to all esoterica
This reality is the one we're stuck with
Until we sleep to graduate to the next one

So why pursue any concern
Except gawking at that sexy lily
Right in the grass in front of you
Or peering at greenery on nearby ranges
Maybe even microscope or telescope views
Since the light of the body
Will only be with you
A little while longer

CARE FOR THE LAND

"Care for the land,
And the land will care for you."
These were the words
A Hawaiian mama shared.
Wherever you stand,
You have now heard what to do.
If you refuse,
Then your soul may not be spared.

ADULT TEETH

You may beg to differ
And I differ too
But the ways you're different
Are not truly you
And my separate flavor
Isn't really me
When with paining biting bane
Differences flee
In the distant memories
Or loneliness you bear
In the difficulties
Of a drink we share

But

Adult teeth
A milk leak
Of an unknown question
Unwritable answer released
A new leaf
A relief
"Individual soul in eternal peace"
Becoming the one, the self-sum

We're all united when it's done

To be brief

Come and differ with me

Shun the rhythm thief

Sink into the meat

Adult teeth

COME ON DOWN

Come on down
Leave a town and weave a river way
Come on down
Be with me, we'll drown the frowns away
Come on down
Wind between the vines of shady mind
Come on down
Find the River, leave a town behind

BY THEIR FRUITS

By their fruits you may know them
They're one with their fruits
From their roots they bestowed them
In sandals or boots

I am not a divider
Though arguments come
Drink and swallow their cider
And mix in their rum

Sugar cane and tobacco
Grew pain in the gain
Called happiness "wacko"
Contentment "insane"

The fruit of the "stop" tree
Will make a comeback
Its yield is not paltry
Abundance, no lack

ENGLISH HAIKU 1

Found among the weeds
Delectable flavor globe
Thank the rowdy weeds

NOTHING

What's really needed today is
        Nothing

We must prepare for tomorrow's
        Nothing

Higher standards of living
        Will come and then go
Going, doing and earning
        Today, tomorrow
It signifies nothing

What do I see behind you?
What matters beyond you?
What's pressing besides the ember inside?
        Nothing.

CLIMBING'S TOO EASY

Climbing's too easy
You're born halfway up a ladder
So, what goes further?
Letting go

Climbing's too easy
When sipping the milk of Bible words
And a mess below may offend you
Forgive me

Once or twice I lost my grip
While gulping direct from the Source
An overflow splashed around too much
Now I can only sit in puddles

Slurp up the messy
Life-juice through my words

A LOVE THAT MINGLES

A love that mingles with the pain
Beats the trinket-giving kind
But Love erasing every gain
Is the one you really want

You thought you wanted this or that in life
Until you felt the edge
Brushing your skin
Whispering to an inner light
Of a puzzling, obliterating whirlwind of delight

While you still have a chance
Abandon all trinkets
To find this pearl
This Joy

SQUEEZE

Only squeeze the essence
Let words fall through the sieve
Spread the Rumi-nations
Recognizing where you live

I wore the plates of a piercer before
A trophy cup was my aim
The stern and principled jacket I wore
To play a breaking-through game

A Kevlar attitude never holds up
When life comes squeezing you down
When death comes piercing to shatter a cup
And leave you spread on the ground

NINE TENTHS

Nine tenths of what I write
Lands in the trash can

Twenty-five languages die
Every year, I hear

For years you wander and pace
Trying to read, to reach
Between the lines
Failing to find
A steady rhyme
Nine tenths of the time

And each
Dead page in the can
Tongue lost without trace
Won't rhyme with your plan
But held a beautiful place

JUST BREATHE, DAD

Just breathe, dad, breathe it out
Kids don't mean to trash the house
Or smash the peace of mind
They only seek to seize
Each moment of living, squeeze
Every drop of laughing glee
They need to learn to breathe
And I must learn to be
More like them, I find

I LIVE AT A PLACE

I live at a place of crossing over
I sit and I face a bridge
A mistress I cannot keep away from
So empty and full I live

My pen will not write until I please her
The enemy has no name
I spear him to cross the bridge and meet her
She's emptying out my shame

It's never a riddle, not a word game
It's not that an evil's dead
The spilling of guts is crossing over
To fill her temple, not my head

I live at a place of crossing over
I sit and I face a bridge
A mistress I cannot keep away from
So empty and full I live

A CURSE ON HIM

A curse on him who ravishes
The forest where my spirit sits.
His work will all go up in smoke;
His days will be a gloomy joke;
His sleepless nights will howl in vain;
My worms will eat his greedy brain.
May emptiness consume his food,
His life become a bitter mood.
Centennial oaks of Riverton
Will shade him not from scorching sun.
May endless horrors haunt his head.
He'll wear the clothing of the dead.
May such a curse be never worn.
May such a man be never born.

IF I WILL NOT

If I will not shine
I'll be the darkness itself
Bring to me what's mine
Don't shadow the lamp on a shelf
Oh bring me your eyes
They're of me, and mine are of you
My sins and your lies
To one in what's perfectly true
Oh come to the light
Come see in these trees where it glows
Awake overnight
To look at a dawning that grows

"RIVER BURN"

We roughly learn to leave
      The past behind
But from back there
      Yet it breathes
Down our necks
      Yours and mine

Back then before I met
      The one I love
You drew me out
      To taste and get
My raging fire
      The sun above

This flavor may not be
      My wife's favorite
Never again
      For you and me
Will bodies touch
      To savor it

You burned in life so hard
      And likely you

Have gone to waste
        To go discard
The savage beauty
        That I knew

We wanted to reclaim
        That river burn
Until the evil
        Spoiled our aim
I fizzled out
        To live and learn

NEARLY DIRTY POEM

When two or three
Including me
Go run in sun all fun and free
We'll spare the boots
Wear bathing suits
We'll tear out there in bare cahoots
Smell wild dill
Feel quiet thrill
Until you yell and take a spill
Girl, skip along
Till scuppernong
Will trip and grip and rip your thong
I will not stand
To lend a hand
Unless you guess you need a man

CENTERED

Centered

A moment
Between a chalice ecstasy
And sunny sheer severity

Swinging
Pendulum in the middle

Balance game between
Holy body flowing wine
And higher planes of mind

Come back here repeatedly
Come back down to this to be

Centered

RIVER PEACE

The brightest word is still
Only secondhand.
The truest writing only tills
Soil of holy land.

So ride the verbs to where
Finally they cease
In empty and aware
Find the River Peace.

ALL BOUND IN BELIEFS AND BEHAVIORS

All bound in beliefs and behaviors
May be one way to be;
The wrong and the right and savior blood
And secondhand knowledge is free.

But narrow and tiny the portal,
A needle's eye in size,
With bits of it written—burned the rest—
"Repent and make heaven the prize."

"Behavior's the portal," said Peter.
"Belief is it," said Paul.
"You know god is Love," old John piped up,
But Thomas remembered it all.

From Mount Olivet misquoted,
The Man, the Myth, the Son—
The mystics who brought him myrrh had seen
Old bindings all coming undone.

WHAT CAN BE SAID?

What can be said?
It's all been said before.
How do you feel?
It's all been felt before.
My work and words
Carry just a little weight,
Less real significance,
Even still less original quality.
Squirming earth is old hat.
Shining light weighs nothing.
What's to be done?
Oh, nothing too important;
But the only thing on earth that satisfies
Down to the core
Is to do it.

HARDWOOD REQUIREMENT

The hot ground wants
A hardwood tree;
If there is one
Then let it be.
But if she's bare
Then put one in
To cool her air
And shade her skin.

Your wife may want
A hardwood man;
If you're still one
Do what you can.
But if she grew
Beyond your shade,
Would other hard-
Wood games be played?

AND FINALLY, A HIGHER GUIDE

And finally, a higher guide
Has found a hearing here,
Still quiet sitting by my side
And flowing in my ear.
Don't ever let them tell you no;
They bar the ocean's tide;
They'll want to tell you where to go
But they don't know Inside.
They strain a gnat and gulp a book
And tell you what to think.
But find a forest, stop and look;
No paper and no ink.
I'm one of them, just now and then;
Don't take it all from me.
My rude addiction is a pen.
The woods, they set me free.

FOUR PERCEPTIONS

On days so gray and overcast
Comes over me a breathing past
A Cymric tongue, a Nordic vein
A sense absorbed in drenching rain

On nights so cool of sight and sound
Sheer present here seeps in the ground
Bare clouds and wind are crowding in
A glare and shadow, yang and yin

On brighter mornings I arise
The light of reason in the eyes
The disk that dawns and grows so clear
Can bring a fruitful future near

A warmer night, the square's complete
I lay me down to rest my feet
In this, year three of poetry
Four pillars build a sense of me

NOW IT'S LATE

"Now it's late, dear mother
Shall I make another
Trellis to train or to brace
Vines into preordained shapes"

There were Eve and Abel
Barely even able
To be seen in a molten tale
Or to sip from a golden grail
       Squeeze a few grapes
       Vines to be shaped

Sober Moses got to learning
How to shape acacia burning
       Breaking a calf of gold
       Making a verbal mold
Molten souls are roughly trained
Now it's late in metal rain

And a mold was cracked when lines were crossed
       Till the cross became the mold
People's gold was found but vines were lost
       In the way a story's told

Crack the trellis

Laughing and laughing and

Break a smile

Up from the abdomen

Hearty and deep was the sound

Waking the sheep all around

WHAT'S FAITH GOT TO DO

What's faith got to do with me and you?
One faith comes up from another's rootstock
And yet another sprouts as a seedling
Pollinated by still other plants
There's a whole damn forest
And so what if one tree is stronger than others
Among the trees go people, good, bad, indecisive
Some climb, some lie down by roots
Others just picnic in the shade
Some prefer open meadows of science
So don't sit on your one branch thinking
That I'm so wrong because I'm not where you are
God is the tree, and the air, and the soil
God is the sunshine, the ocean, me and you floating
We're like spores of mold attached to the God tree
And we're here, and behold, it's good

THERE IS NO DESCRIBING

There is no describing possible
Of the tunnel you descend
If and when the light you bubbled from
Sucks you in to be your Friend

Words won't touch Creator energy
Essence of the gurgling spring
Though a few may jog the memory
And the memory makes you sing

DARKNESS AND BRIGHTNESS

Darkness and brightness
Go swirling around
Here in a puddle
Down here on the ground

What you were doing
For just a few years
Can't bar your being
From clearing the fears

Tears may go swirling
In laughter it steams
Muddy old mixing
And grabbing your dreams

HEAVY CLIMB

"The hall of Gynddylan is dark this evening"
And "Absolom, oh Absolom, my son"
The sound of grief and a heavy weeping

The tale of a soul in pain and pining
And laboring and laboring to climb
Out of the soil, into the shining

AND THE SLEEPTALKING

And the sleeptalking old boy whispered,
 "Give me your paranoia,
 Your harrowing dysphoria,
 Your words wielded as clubs,
 Blinders, excesses, and snubs,
 Storms which have seen their own day;
 My jar of fireflies will light your way."

WHEN YOU FIND

When you find the portion of earth that holds
Your passion and peace intertwined
In her lines—each cranny and nook and hole,
Then heaven and earth are combined.

When you mind her healing and steep your soul
In feeling her beat to the bone,
Then a binding rhythm can make you whole
And purify all you have known.

When your heart is dipped in her river mist,
Your sunburn is soothed in her balm,
You'll release the hand where you held a fist
And your mind will be full of her calm.

THIS SOIL IN WAGRAM

This soil in Wagram is –
      My God – she's so
Right, and dark, and flirty
And fate has stated I'm –
      Though not born here –
Here reborn all dirty

An awestruck man, he stands
Relinquishment in hand
      While death and downpour take a turn
      To darken like a charcoal burn
Fair soil he called his own
A sandy gentle loam

When empty big ones say
      "Go big or go home"
Recall how full this homeland
And there she's lying back
      A curvy grove
Snug among the farmland

And nevermore may pen-song be
About my strength, nor tools, nor me

Now arising only by her joy
Her pleasant use of my shovel-toy
Her body, tender body of
A flowing stream, or leaves above
The milky way, the moving skies
The mingled taste of tangled lives
    And upward mobility is a load of bull
    When natural borders enclose a field so full
    Look what they're moving up away from
Limitations bound in a sacred song
This sound, these ripples here unfurling
Of this ground, this light and darkness swirling
This silent singing mayhem
This soil here in Wagram

PRICKLY PEOPLE

Prickly people
Like prickly vines
May get their way a while
But are prone to getting cut down
Just when they think they've made it

The way you treat the land
And the way you treat your neighbors
Is the way God will be with you

Maybe life was rough
Forced them to be so thorny
As thorny is the crown they place
And thorny also will be
Their comeuppance

HOW DO YOU MEASURE

How do you measure happiness?
You don't,
Not if you're fine enough inside.
The growth rings are in there;
No call to cut and count them all.

Happy folks don't fell centuries-old trees
For convenience or "a better view"
Or to install a gas station.

Happy folks know
No matter who you are
Someone somewhere would love to
Do happy things to your body.
And that feeling won't be measured
And that ought to make you smile inside.

MY MUSE IS A GARDEN

My muse is a garden
Community garden
To care for her dirt and to share in her work
Together with others
Some hard-working others
With tools she is eyeing on days when I shirk

They'll dig and they'll tease her
Then fertilize, please her
To see how her soil is alive in their sweat
And there as we share her
And none of us spare her
Fertility's singing the best poem yet

INTO CHURNING CHAOS

Into churning chaos
Order
      Until
      Order goes off balance
      Overreaching
      Then old timing
Brings into the order
Chaos

Anyone can spoil it
Only
      The friends
      Mend, create, and heal it
      Woe to those who
      Only know to
Add into a current
Chaos

WHAT'S A LIFETIME FOR?

What's a lifetime for?
    To love the work;
    To work the love.
Who could ask for more?
    Turn hands to roots.
    Turn eyes above.
Though here and there we look too far
Or shed a tear or climb too hard,
    We're here below;
    We, lowly doves.

I gave them the key to the kingdom already;
They lost it within a discussion too empty.
The boot wasn't right and the foot wasn't steady;
And climbing their hill couldn't possibly tempt me.

Go climb until you've had your fill,
    But love is handiwork.
    Be hands for working love.
So, slide down here and maybe we'll
    Be living in the work,
    Be friends, be hand in glove.

TREES AND MISTAKES

His live oak thrives under the shade
Of nodding stately pine
Where pondering mistakes we made
Becomes a job of mine.
Her tulip poplar didn't take
In that bare sunny spot;
Demurred, preferred a swamp or lake,
But there we let it rot.
She needed healing, so I gave
Some words I felt may work.
And voila! I became a knave
A crook, an ass, a jerk.
The bare and open honesty
Of someone's son-in-law
Was doomed (it darkly dawned on me)
To be a glaring flaw.
But now our olive tree is where
Her tulip used to be.
The olive loves the sun and air
Of open honesty.

ONCE THEY'RE NEGLECTED

Once they're neglected for just a year
Some of these trails disappear.
Each of them calls me, but when I'm there
Sons may decide I just don't care.

Clipping can wait while I skip this mile
Loud and excited with my child.
Poems may grow from his chaos, too,
Just as the tangled trails can do.

THE CAVE IS STILL

The cave is still in there
Intact
Just filled up with water
In fact
Where water music stills the soul
Like water flows to fill a hole
Like floating in a fluid womb
Like sleeping in a swampy tomb
While they on the outside
Spin dry
Each spider and cricket
And fly

WHAT DO THEY SIGNIFY?

What do they signify,
These torrents of words?
Currents are for riding loosely,
Flowing in and out on irregular rhythm
Like straddling a paddleboard in
The shallow stream of life.
How cute when some of us
Care so much for so many things,
Holding so tightly.
What do we think we'll gain?
Serious tones don't need to mean tight concern
And words flow where they want to go.
Loosely might the waves be ridden,
Loosely as the river of life
Downstream irrevocably between the banks
Of space and time.
Thoughts fail here.
Each spurt and eddy signifies no more
Than life itself.

YOU LIKE?

You like the trappings of affluent status?
You like those manicured yards?
The golf and collars and jewelry dinners,
The never showing your cards?

      And softer hands
      And stocks and lands
      And cars and boats
      Cigars and votes
      Leaders' impunities
      Gated immunities

Enjoy the daydreams that seem to last.
      What swells too much will deflate.
So, as you're puffing above the past,
      Look back before it's too late.

MONEY IS A GAME

Money is a game,
A twisted joke;
Dangles there to make you chase it,
Then it goes to smoke.

Saw a shiny thing,
Went after it
Till it tripped and tied your feet up,
Scrambled all your wit.

Luxuries are there
For you to win;
In them life and all its beauty
Scatter in the wind.

ON DAYS OF CLARITY

On days of clarity
When moments are mature
And all is there to see
We find that less is more

And then return the nights
Of heavy humid air
When dew has fogged the sights
In dimness everywhere

Though less is more, it's true
The nights are truer still
Forgetting all we knew
Of life we'll never get our fill

IT'S A SHAME

It's a shame when drive-thrus are
      Anonymous.
If you stop and think too hard
      You're losing it.
It's a shame when smartphones are
      The fate you face.
There inside a lonely car
      Who wins the race?
If you just don't make the link
      It's not for you.
Some will float and some will sink;
      You know it's true.
Though transactions come and go,
      No unity.
It's a shame when there is no
      Community.

WHATEVER ACCEPTS

Whatever accepts the life within you
Cannot be the enemy.
Whatever projects the light upon you
Cannot be a heresy.
Whatever reflects the Maker's image
Cannot be idolatry.
Whatever is blessed within a marriage
Cannot be adultery.
The image of shining life that owns you
Depends upon an eye.
And being the channel or the vessel,
Our job until we die.

TO GEORGE MONBIOT

From an amateur soloist standing beside
The choir you're preaching to,
Here's a single note.

Your struggle may be that
When all assumptions boil down,
At rock bottom
What you truly believe in is science.
       Where is your only hope?
              Maths. Engineering. Technology.
       How shall we heal and be saved?
              In embrace and enforcement of
              Such human knowledge.

Good, this is how you study the soil,
But have you *met* her?
If you did
You might come to know
(Please excuse the term)
God.

PAIN IS ONLY

Pain is only inside of time,
But so also is pleasure.
Marking hours, the bell will chime
To make a morbid measure.

Space is only inside of time
And heaven's all the matter.
Race the clock all you want; it's fine,
But pictures here will shatter.

SHOW ME SOMEONE

Show me someone
Who's brutal but generous
Such as the sun.

Sun may create
Interior illuming
Like he makes everything else.

Talk better wait
Shuffled up onto a shelf
Until the unsettling
Silence is great.

       Better to write than talk.
       Better to walk than run.
       Letters of white as chalk
       (Webs like a spider's spun)
       Creep in the head; they stalk,
       Steep in awareness thin,
       Keep tossing thoughts to knock
       On me like children's din,
       Noisily clanging pans
       Past when it might subside.

Data and maths and plans
Crash on me like a tide.

Step number one
Of sunning the consciousness:
Shut up; be done.

I DID NOT INTEND

I did not intend for this pen
To mumble a jumble of mess
It's only to recognize when
A jungle cannot be made less
Where up from below you it comes
That sweet and perpetual song
I cannot abandon the drums
Nor shrink from a chorus so long
We rein it back in here and there
To make it a moral to mold
But out it the swamp, in the air
Is something you never can hold
I'll never be sorry for this
For better or worse let it sing
Allowing each hit and each miss
To be an ephemeral thing
Which circles around and around
Recurs every lifetime or two
To run or to rest in the ground
While flowing from me into you

"CIVILIZATION"

"Civilization"
Set up, almost by design,
For confrontation;
A temporary paradigm

A short-lived species of outgrown tribes
Is burning through all its paradise
It's all downhill when you civilize...

And downhill's a breeze,
So don't get me wrong;
They make better cheese;
Their metal is strong
But "yes sir" and "please"
Have hidden too long
A smothering squeeze
Of harmony gone

"You'll sleep when you're dead,
        Find peace in your head,
                Till then no relief, no release," Satan said.

FOR A "FOREIGNER"

For a "foreigner" who reads
From beyond any ocean or border:
I've been forging all these lines
From a land of bipolar disorder.

Back and forth the hormones go
In the place that I'm calling my nation.
When the pendulum will slow
I don't know; it's an odd situation.

You may go ahead and laugh
At the drama, or cry for the carnage.
But we're not all quite so bad
And we may yet grow out of this garbage.

This is no apology.
New creation is mayhem in stages
And the roots will grow, you see,
As the land of invention finally ages.

WE ARE BUT ONE

We are but one
And "I" am we
Part of the land
The land in me
To feel the way she feels
Create the thing that heals
She moves the way "I" move
There's nothing here to prove
A house is but
A comfort post
So any hut
Can match the most
Ridiculous mansion
So what's the use
Of added expansion
When this profuse
Old union gives
A place forever
To one who lives
In here, together

THE CIRCLE EXPANDS

The circle expands forever
The wheel spins on in force
You'll never describe the center
I can't explain the source

That's the grape I want, not this one
That one way up there, shiny, ripe and juicy
If only I could reach

From pain there arises beauty
A cycle to redeem
Our globe is so blue and fruity
With such a fragile sheen

Such a hazardous vastness
Of frigid chaos out there
Just let me see
And yet be
In here

It's turning around in season
Though often hard to see
Let's not give away our reason
In mystic harmony

HE SHOVED

He shoved and cut in line
And thought it's normal, fine
Because his folk forgot
What's strength and what is not.
His chickens will come in
And those of all his kin
Who roost in loneliness
Recalling only this,
That history is his loss
And poverty a cross
To bear as long as they
Were spending every day
In joy at others' pain
In selfish, grasping gain.
One day he may awake
With nothing left to take.

PERPETUAL FOLD ROLLING

Perpetual fold rolling
Folding into itself away
And flipping and unfolding
Opens, approaching ever this way

Touch it when your eyelids close
But know nobody really knows
How or whether conscious sight
Wakes up if you die tonight

Let the essence
Wax and wane
"I don't know"
Is my refrain

JUST ENOUGH IS BETTER

Just enough is better
Than more and more and more.
Round and round the chasing
Becomes a weary chore.

      Runners may be split in two:
      Some make friends with ticking time,
      Others never really do.
      Every circumstance is sliced,
      Seen depending on the view.

At least that's how the game will go
(Us and them and win and lose)
As long as we no longer know
Where to stop and what to choose.

HOW TINY A PIECE

How tiny a piece
Of nothing I am
And
And yet
How happy a piece
Of everything I am
Ah
Ah yes
Come on, do you sense it?

I'M NOT

I'm not a writer by career.
Professional? Not me.
I'm but repeating what I hear
In silence underneath a tree.

Peculiar senses I relay
May sometimes be my own,
But other times my mind's away
And better lines are freely grown.

It could be called a craft, I guess,
But give the woods their due.
They give and all I say is "yes".
They show you what I never knew.

LOOK HERE

Look here
We have native wisteria
What's it useful for?
For winding beautifully there
Sure, it gets in your way
Makes you work harder
So if you want, you can
Weave it to baskets or chairs
Or make a living rope bridge
But first
Step back and simply
Look here

ESCAPING

Anything you truly gained
Was already latent within you.
Hasten its escaping
With me tonight.

If you steward soil for continuity
It will carry on in perpetuity
As a living force in promiscuity
And a membrane film of generosity
To a steward's mind in reciprocity,
Not to those who tread in animosity.
They never found their
      Escape velocity.

A PLASTIC DISPOSABLE CUP

A plastic disposable cup
Dropped in a sacred grove
Displays how far we have dropped,
How deep into weakness we dove.

A time may arise to clean up
Errors and grievous crimes;
To leave our perching on top,
Rejoining our kin in the vines.

One day they may be codified,
Rights the old woods deserve,
Their honor no longer denied.
One day we may summon the nerve.

LACK OF PATIENCE

Lack of patience for telling stories
Is my excuse
There I dug impatiently, feverishly
Knowing somehow this was the spot
In spurts came clods of life
Damp and aromatic
Worms and critters everywhere
What business could I rightly have in
This sacred place?
But lo and behold
It survives the child's banalities
      Still opening new realities
          As if on the cusp of eternity

One day if a story comes to compel
Well then, my pen will possibly tell
Till then, in here among the stumps
Please excuse my clumsy clumps

THERE STANDS A FERTILE PATCH

There stands a fertile patch
Where Judas met his match.
He's feeding all the mass
Of fungus, bugs and grass.
Worms fill their banquet halls
Where mighty feasters fall.
Fertility's unleashed
When Peter is the feast.
Here lay some fertile brains
Until some summer rains
Undid their separate airs,
Their units and their pairs,
Uniting all the stink
More fully than you think.
While Papa's up today
Continuing his way,
No truth is set in stone
Like Mama on her throne.

OF WHICH BRAND OF FAITH

Of which brand of faith
Are you a consumer?
When they pass the plate
How much do you pay?
And will your reward
Come later or sooner?
Is biology
Permitted today?

TO AN EX

You asked me what I'd really like.
My reply was true:
"Befriending" more than one woman
(No offense to you).
No one else was out there yet;
All I dreamed of was
Just the freedom to say yes.
You could, too, because
One or both, what's fair is fair.
Sharp, you took offense.
This rhyme's childish, I'm aware,
But in my defense...

> *Two, three, four*
> *Four, three, two*
> *She's got more*
> *"Soul" than you*
> *Four, three, two*
> *Two, three, four*
> *One's alright*
> *More is more*

Nothing's better than enough;
Don't need more, *don't need less.*

Waking up to you was rough
(Not your fault, I confess).
One is where it rightly starts
But you weren't the one.
Scrap the flowers and the hearts;
Life was meant for fun.

PURE OPENING

Look up at all those stars
All in one glance
Each so far apart

How can the eye be pure
Until you dare
To open up the heart?

A deep pain grew
Opened a vista
View you never knew

How can a mind be clean
Until it's open
Where creations start?

WHAT'S COMING

I might
One of these nights
Purify my soul
Make my heart right
      You, too
           In advance
                Of what's coming

You thought
The bug they fought
Was a deadly mess
An ordeal fraught
      But no
           It's child's play
                To what's coming

ADAM IS DEAD

Adam is dead
Long live Adam
Prometheus, give up the fire

That thing you sense
Can't be spoken
No words in the root of desire

Layers below
No one knows them
They're stacking a funeral pyre

CHICKEN BARRACKS

Oh, he owns a "chicken farm" does he

You mean one of those concentration camps?

I've seen what the fowl are born to do

  Run and peck and try to fly

  Underneath His good blue sky

    Roosting in bushes and trees

    Feeling a heavenly breeze

  So that when you eat

  You're not poisoning yourself

Like we poison the word "farm"

By attaching it to

Those abominable

Ugly

Smelly

Unrhyming

Monstrous

Barracks

TO THE BUILDERS OF THE GAS STATION

What did our oak tree ever do?
Cut off a tidy highway view?
He bore no fault, but what of you?
    A century or so he stood;
    For one or two more he was good.
    What will they do with all his wood?
        Some local ancestors were there
        To love his shade and breathe his air.
        Who smothers them had best beware.
    We hold no hot animosity,
    But hate the fate of the stately tree
    And cry for criminal cruelty.
Now to atone for such a sin,
Come put three younger oak trees in;
Until you do, you'll never win.

        The minds who "own" this land, I pray,
        Will end their crimes and mend their way,
        Or hold the bag on judgement day.

RAIN, RAIN, RAIN

Rain, rain, rain

Beautiful, beautiful, beautiful

Rain, rain, rain

Down, bring a drink to a thirsty ground

Feeding the greenery all around

Working a wonderful rhythm sound

Washing off some pain

Soak, flow, ever abound

Come, drum, drain

Beautiful, beautiful, beautiful

Rain, rain, rain

OCTOBER 10TH

From juglone juice my hands are black;
I stain my boots, I strain my back
In hunting down the fragrant globes
Of black walnuts in holy groves.

I bless the one who cherishes
A meadow as it perishes
In giving way to trees of nuts;
May more each day fall down for us.

At dawn, day ten of October
We call an end, the hunt's over.
A month or two we did our best.
Our squirrel cousins get the rest.

WHEN IT'S THE TIME

When it's the time to die
You die
There's One that marks the time
Not I
Though man may stoop to do
The deed
All fear will fail when you
Concede
That whether hard or soft
It comes
So go with head aloft
      For you we'll tap the drums

LIMITED?

Limited by humble tools
And that's the point of them
Self-limitation of us fools
In reverence, amen
   If you think that everything
   Is or ought to be
   Explicable, I weep for you.
   I hope one day you'll see....
Okay, I may have somewhat lied;
My ego hasn't flat-out died.
   And even though I hate
   To raise an ugly fence,
   Don't let me overstate
   My lack of arrogance.
I crown myself a king upon "my soil"
And grease my tomahawk in olive oil.
   I take my work too seriously
   In solitude, deliriously
So sit me down and share a drink
And tell me what you really think.

ANOTHER WAY

Falling from above
Surging from below
Timing wasn't ours
Heavy was a flow
Out into the books
Emptied out my soul
Now to hold my peace
Lean into the role
Of a quiet friend
Fewer things to say
This won't be the end
Just another way

And a couple of Welsh efforts...

CERDD GYMRAEG GYNTAF
(FIRST WELSH POEM)

Nid oedd fy nghoed yn hen

Ond rhywbeth yn eu awel...

Mae cylch yn nodi'r tawel.

Collais fy modrwy wen

Yr ail o Fai – Fy mhen!

Cloddiais a thorri llwybrau

Yno gerllaw eu gwreiddiau

Nes i amser ddod i ben.

AIL CERDD GYMRAEG
(SECOND WELSH POEM)

Ni allaf ei esbonio

Y dderwen i'm llygaid

Golwg ar harddwch bywyd

Mor anfeidrol, sanctaidd

Ni allaf ei ddisgrifio

Mae'r dagrau'n dod i lawr

Gallwn i eistedd yma am byth

Mae'r rhyfeddod mor fawr

Ni allaf ddianc ohono

Llygaid disglair y blaidd

Yno mewn cysgod cyfnewidiol

Mor anfeidrol, sanctaidd